THE OFFIC...
HEART OF
MIDLOTHIAN
ANNUAL 2024

Written by Neil Hobson and Jamie McIntosh
Designed by Lucy Boyd

g

A Grange Publication

© 2023. Published by Grange Communications Ltd., Edinburgh, under licence from Heart of Midlothian. Printed in the EU.

Photographs © James Christie, David Mollison, Robert Doyle, SNS Group

ISBN 978-1-915879-21-9

CONTENTS

Hello, and welcome to The Official
HEART OF MIDLOTHIAN ANNUAL 2024

As captain of this fantastic football club, it gives me great pleasure to welcome you to this year's annual. 2022/23 was a season that will be remembered by all who hold this club dear to their heart. On the pitch, we had derby triumphs and European adventures in countries a long way from home.

We stood together when we hit bumps in the road, and of course, the year also presented challenges for me on a personal level.

My season came to a premature end after breaking my leg in a game against Dundee United at Tannadice on Christmas Eve 2022. It was a bad injury but one I'm working very hard to come back from. Nothing would give me greater pride than pulling on a Hearts jersey once again, and I'll do everything I can to get back out on the pitch at Tynecastle.

Whilst we always have an eye on the future, and all of the exciting things to come, it's appropriate to reflect on the past as Heart of Midlothian celebrates its 150th anniversary season. It's fitting we acknowledge the history and people behind this institution, from the early days of the club's inception right through to the modern era. Contained within the pages of this annual, we'll chart a century and a half of triumph, tragedy, adventures, and adversity as we made our way through history and to the top of the Scottish game.

It has, and continues to be, a privilege to be a part of this club's story. It's up to us, you and every subsequent generation of Hearts supporter to write the next chapter. Who knows what it'll bring, but I can't wait to be along for the journey.

This is our story; this is our song.

Craig Gordon
Club Captain, Heart of Midlothian

SEASON REVIEW

JULY

Season 22/23 began at Tynecastle as Hearts welcomed Malky Mackay's Ross County to Gorgie.

This was the men in maroon's first competitive outing of the new season, whereas their opponents had already featured in the League Cup group stages, and it showed, as County looked by far the sharper of the two sides in the early exchanges.

The Jambos eased themselves into the game however, and they took the lead on the hour mark thanks to Alan Forrest. Barrie McKay made sure of the points 13 minutes from time, before Jordan White ensured a nervy ending would take place, as he volleyed home after being sent clean through on Craig Gordon.

Hearts held their nerve though to record an opening day victory.

AUGUST

August started with a trip to Easter Road and just when it looked like Lawrence Shankland's first goal in maroon would seal a derby victory, Martin Boyle popped up to equalise in the final moment and rescue a point for Hibs.

Back at Tynecastle, and Hearts made it two home wins out of two as they hammered a struggling Dundee United 4-1.

The Jam Tarts got off to the perfect start as Shankland bagged the opening goal inside a minute, before second-half strikes from Barrie McKay, Jorge Grant and Josh Ginnelly rounded off a comfortable afternoon in Gorgie.

Next up, Hearts travelled to Switzerland to take on FC Zürich in the first leg of the Europa League Play-off.

A first-half penalty from Shankland had Hearts ahead in the pouring rain, but Zürich completed a second-half comeback to take a lead to Edinburgh for the second leg seven days later.

With one eye on the second leg of the Europa League Play-off, the last thing Hearts wanted was a trip to Celtic Park. A much-changed 11 took to the field in the East End of Glasgow as Celtic ran out 2-0 winners in a match that saw Hearts finish with nine men on the field, following the late dismissals of Alex Cochrane and Toby Sibbick.

Back at Tynecastle, and Hearts produced arguably one of their best performances of the season against the then Swiss champions.

In the first 45 minutes, Hearts did everything but score as they battered Zurich at a raucous Tynecastle. The game turned nine minutes after the break as Jorge Grant was shown a second yellow card and the Swiss side made their man advantage count, as they went on to win the match 1-0 and send Hearts into the Europa Conference League group stages.

Back in domestic action and Hearts continued their good home form with a pulsating 3-2 victory over St Johnstone. Graham Carey gave the Perth Saints an early advantage, but goals from Kye Rowles, Liam Boyce and a late penalty from Shankland ensured three points.

It was a bittersweet afternoon however, as Liam Boyce was substituted in the first half and was ruled out for the remainder of the season. Kye Rowles was also injured when bundling the ball home from close range and was ruled out for nine weeks with a fractured metatarsal.

Hearts ended a busy August in League Cup action with Kilmarnock the visitors to Tynecastle. It was fair to say Hearts had bigger fish to fry at this stage of the season, but it was still a disappointing result as Hearts' League Cup heartbreak continued with Innes Cameron netting the only goal of the game as Killie ran out 1-0 winners.

SEPTEMBER

September began at the Tony Macaroni where a Christian Montano strike was enough to hand the Lions all three points in a game where Hearts never really got going.

The games were coming thick and fast at this stage and Hearts were dealt a real sickener when Istanbul Basaksehir pitched up at Tynecastle and did a job on the Jambos. The classy Turks ran out 4-0 winners in the opening Conference League group stage match.

Hearts headed to Latvia next to take on RFS, knowing full well that anything other than three points would likely make qualification from the group a near impossible task.

That man Shankland again delivered from the penalty spot to give Hearts a half-time lead and after soaking up a lot of pressure in the second half, a classic counter-attack resulted in Alan Forrest wrapping up the three points and kickstarting a memorable evening for the travelling Jambos in the Latvian capital.

From Latvia to Lanarkshire, as Hearts ended September at Fir Park. It is never easy to bring your A-game on the Sunday after an away match in Europe on the Thursday, but the men in maroon picked up three precious points in a clinical 3-0 victory.

The heroes in Riga were again on target, as Shankland opened the scoring before a second-half brace from Forrest added some gloss to the scoreline.

OCTOBER

October turned out to be a tough month for the Jambos, and it got off to the worst possible start as Rangers defeated Hearts 4-0 at Tynecastle.

An early brace from Antonio Colak had the Gers in command, even before the straight red card shown to Cammy Devlin. Ryan Kent and Alfredo Morelos struck late on, on a frustrating afternoon in Gorgie.

Fiorentina were then the visitors to Tynecastle five days later. The classy Italians ran out comfortable 3-0 winners in what was a hammer-blow to Hearts' hopes of qualification.

Three days later, Hearts were in Ayrshire to take on Kilmarnock. The Jambos found themselves two goals down with half an hour remaining, but Stephen Humphrys halved the deficit to set the stage for Nathaniel Atkinson to step forward and lash home a volley from the edge of the box in the 94th minute.

The Jam Tarts were back on European business with a trip to Florence. Hearts fans flocked to Italy in their numbers, but even the Hearts fans couldn't stop Fiorentina from following-up their comfortable win at Tynecastle with an even more professional performance on home soil.

Hearts were four down at the break, but showed some spirit in the second half as Stephen Humphrys gave the Gorgie Boys something to shout about as Fiorentina ran out 5-1 winners.

The big games kept on coming for Hearts as they faced a gruelling trip north to face Aberdeen. Strikes from Duk and Vicente Besuijen saw the Dons run out 2-0 winners.

Hearts would have been grateful to be back at Tynecastle the following weekend, this time for a showdown with Celtic. In a seven-goal thriller, VAR made its Tynecastle debut. It was the visitors who ran out 4-3 winners, despite a hat-trick from Lawrence Shankland. It was a crazy game in which Hearts were ahead and behind but a late strike from Greg Taylor saw all three points head along the M8 to Glasgow.

Next up, Hearts welcomed RFS to Tynecastle in the final home game of their European swan song. The Jambos came flying out the traps and were two goals to the good after just 12 minutes thanks to goals from Shankland and Andy Halliday.

RFS pulled one back before half-time and it was a nervy finish as Hearts began to tire, but the men in maroon held on to the three points to ensure they would finish third in their group.

Three days later, Hearts faced another long journey, but this time up to Dingwall to face Ross County. Jordan White had County ahead early doors but just like on Thursday night, Shankland and Halliday came up with the goods to ensure Hearts ended a testing month on a high.

NOVEMBER

Hearts started November in Istanbul as they closed out their European campaign. It was a young Hearts side as Lewis Neilson, Connor Smith and Euan Henderson all featured from the start.

With the Jambos trailing 3-0, in the dying embers, Nathaniel Atkinson popped up with a goal to ensure Hearts ended their European journey with something to cheer about as the Turks ran out 3-1 winners to top the group.

With the European campaign now over, it was all eyes on the league as Hearts looked to guarantee European football in some form, for the following season.

Motherwell were the visitors to Tynecastle in another pulsating encounter.

Jorge Grant was shown a straight red card after just 34 minutes which left Hearts with an uphill task, but they went down the tunnel at half-time with a slender lead thanks to Andy Halliday.

Just two minutes into the second half, Halliday added his second and from that point onwards, it was time for Hearts to protect their lead.

Motherwell were always going to get chances with the man advantage and Louis Moult halved the deficit from the penalty spot just after the hour and when Blair Spittal equalised 10 minutes from time, it was set to be a nervy ending.

In a dramatic twist, Hearts were awarded a penalty in the final minute of normal time, and with Shankland standing over it, there was never really any doubt about the outcome.

Ahead of the World Cup break, the fixture schedule was becoming extremely congested. Hearts were at Ibrox three days later, where there was a welcome return to the starting line-up for Kye Rowles, although the Aussie's presence wasn't enough to stop Rangers as a second-half strike from Malik Tillman saw the Gers run out narrow victors.

In the final match before the World Cup break, Hearts welcomed Livingston to Tynecastle. In what was proving to be a recurring theme, it was another dramatic afternoon at Tynecastle.

The West Lothian side went ahead ten minutes after the break, through Sean Kelly and when Stephen Kelly missed the chance to double the visitors' lead from the penalty spot after being brought down by Rowles, who was shown a straight red card; Hearts were buoyant.

In what had been a really tough season, what with injuries and added fixture congestion, there was a real togetherness around Tynecastle, and the roof nearly came off the stadium when Josh Ginnelly rifled home a 97th-minute equaliser to send Hearts into the break on a high.

DECEMBER

Five weeks later, and domestic football was back with Kilmarnock making the trip to Tynecastle. Hearts were on top from the start and goals from Ginnelly and Shankland had Hearts on easy street before the half-hour mark.

Ash Taylor pulled one back for the visitors 17 minutes from time, before Shankland sealed all three points in the final minute of normal time from the penalty spot.

Hearts were at Tannadice on Christmas Eve as that man Shankland was again the hero with an ice-cool penalty in stoppage time to rescue a point for the Jambos.

Hearts were behind twice as goals from Stephen Fletcher and Dylan Levitt had United ahead, but Michael Smith ensured the sides were level at the break, before Shankland stepped up with the final kick of the game to restore parity.

It wasn't all festive cheer however, as Craig Halkett hobbled off in the early stages and in the second half, captain Craig Gordon suffered a double leg-break. Both wouldn't feature again for the remainder of the season.

The Jambos were again on the road following the festivities as they travelled up to Perth looking to register their first league win at McDiarmid Park since 2010.

Kevin Kyle scored a penalty for the Jambos that afternoon and Shankland followed suit by opening the scoring from the spot after just 14 minutes.

Alan Forrest had the Jambos on easy street after 33 minutes and just when it looked like that Perth victory was finally going to arrive, relatively stress-free, Stevie May halved the deficit for Saints from the spot.

Barrie McKay came off the bench to restore Hearts' two-goal lead in fine fashion, and although Jamie Murphy ensured a nervy ending by pulling one back ten minutes from time, Hearts held on for a vital away win.

JANUARY

The New Year began with a Tynecastle Edinburgh derby as Hearts hammered their rivals 3-0 thanks to a first-half brace from Lawrence Shankland, before Stephen Humphrys added a third in stoppage time.

Hearts then travelled to Paisley for the first match of a double-header with St Mirren. Ryan Strain had the Buddies ahead inside the opening five minutes, but an in-swinging cross deceived everyone waiting in the box and looped past Trevor Carson to ensure the spoils were shared.

Six days later the sides met at Tynecastle, where a first-half strike from Barrie McKay was enough to see the points remain in Gorgie.

Aberdeen were the next visitors to Tynecastle, and they were thrashed 5-0 by a rampant Hearts side who were four goals to the good at half-time.

A brace from Josh Ginnelly, a goal-of-the-season contender from Michael Smith and the customary Shankland penalty sealed a memorable midweek night win at Tynecastle.

Scottish Cup action next up and what feels like an inevitability these days, Hearts were paired with their Edinburgh rivals in the Fourth Round.

Josh Ginnelly had Hearts ahead at the break after volleying home from inside the box, before Shankland took centre stage to become the first Hearts player to score 20 goals in a season since John Robertson in the 1991/92 campaign.

Shanks himself probably couldn't have imagined it any better. A neat layoff from Stephen Humphrys, allowed the number nine to open up his body and fire a volley perfectly into the bottom corner, sending the Jambos behind the goal wild.

And as if that wasn't enough, Toby Sibbick charged up field in the 90th minute and dinked the ball over David Marshall to add a third, before producing a celebration that will be remembered for years to come.

Seven days later and Hearts were back in West Lothian to face Livingston. As often appears to be the case at the Tony Macaroni, it was a close affair in which the sides couldn't be separated. Both sides did have chances with Hearts new boys Garang Kuol and Yutaro Oda getting close, but it ended scoreless.

FEBRUARY

The shortest month of the year started with a visit from Rangers.

The Gers arrived at Tynecastle and won convincingly thanks to goals from Malik Tillman and a brace from Alfredo Morelos.

Hearts responded well to that defeat by defeating Dundee United at Tynecastle three days later. They did it the hard way after Stephen Fletcher put the Tangerines ahead inside ten minutes, but the game flipped when Ryan Edwards was shown a straight red card on the half-hour mark.

The men in maroon took their time, but goals in the final 20 minutes from Lawrence Shankland and Alex Cochrane put Hearts ahead, before Stephen Humphrys' outrageous goal-of-the-season winner in the final minute sealed the points in style.

Humps received a pass inside his own half and after seeing Mark Birighitti off his line, let fly with his left foot. The keeper had no chance and had to watch, as the ball flew over him and into the back of the net.

After their victory over Hibernian, Hearts were handed a Friday night trip to Hamilton in the Scottish Cup Fifth Round. A goal in each half from Stephen Humphrys and Cammy Devlin ensured a comfortable 2-0 win for the men in maroon.

Sadly, Hearts continued to struggle on the road in the league as they were beaten by Motherwell at Fir Park. Goals either side of half-time from Jonathan Obika and Blair Spittal gave the Steelmen all three points.

MARCH

Back at Tynecastle though, Hearts had no such issues. St Johnstone were the next team to be put to the sword as Josh Ginnelly continued to thrive in the central striker role, his brace had Hearts coasting before Jorge Grant added a third to round off a comfortable home win.

A midweek trip to Celtic Park was next for the Jambos and although they went ahead through Josh Ginnelly and ultimately competed with the runaway leaders for large spells, Celtic proved too strong in the end as goals from Daizen Maeda, Kyogo and Sead Hakšabanović saw Celtic run out 3-1 winners.

The sides met again three days later, and the Hoops again emerged victorious, this time in the Scottish Cup at Tynecastle. First-half strikes from Aaron Mooy and Kyogo had Celtic ahead before Cameron Carter-Vickers added a third as Hearts exited the cup at the quarter-final stage.

Next up, Hearts were at Pittodrie. The Dons were three ahead after 28 minutes and never looked back on a frustrating afternoon for the men in maroon.

APRIL

Hearts' away struggles continued in April as despite going ahead through Lawrence Shankland, the Jambos were defeated 2-1 at Rugby Park as a penalty from Dan Armstrong and a strike from Christian Doidge gave Killie a huge three points in their battle to survive the drop.

Back at Tynecastle, Hearts welcomed Stephen Robinson's St Mirren to Gorgie as they looked to receive a much-needed boost to take into the following weekend's Edinburgh derby.

It wasn't to be however, as despite dominating possession, Hearts couldn't make an early breakthrough and St Mirren capitalised as strikes from Curtis Main and Mark O'Hara gave the Paisley Saints their first win at Tynecastle since 2013.

That match turned out to be Robbie Neilson's final match in charge. He was replaced by former Hearts captain Steven Naismith on an interim basis.

It was too quick a turnaround to notice any real difference and in a game that lacked quality, it was Hibs who came up with the match-winning moment as Kevin Nisbet's strike midway through the second half proved to be the only goal of the game.

Hearts were back at Tynecastle for their final game before the split, with Ross County the visitors for an early kick-off in front of the Sky Sports cameras.

When he was appointed, Naismith had promised an attacking brand of football and the Jambos certainly delivered on that that afternoon as first-half strikes from Alex Cochrane, Josh Ginnelly and two from Shankland had the men in maroon four goals to the good at the break.

Shankland bagged his hat-trick in the second half and Ginnelly also added his second of the afternoon in a 6-1 thrashing of the Staggies.

MAY

The split began with Hearts hosting Celtic. The Jambos were in good spirits following the Ross County result and they started on the front foot, but the game changed when Alex Cochrane was shown a straight red card in the final minute of the first half.

Hearts worked hard after the interval, but Kyogo fired Celtic ahead midway through the second half before Oh added a second ten minutes from time.

The men in maroon were exposed in Paisley the following weekend. St Mirren raced into a 2-0 half-time lead thanks to goals from Joe Shaughnessy and Ryan Strain.

Josh Ginnelly gave Hearts hope 17 minutes from time and although Peter Haring was shown a straight red card, which was later reduced to a yellow upon appeal, it was down to that man Shankland to rescue Hearts with a 96th-minute penalty to ensure the spoils were shared.

Hearts welcomed Aberdeen to Tynecastle the following weekend and again, they came from behind to avoid defeat.

Mattie Pollock headed the Dons into a first half lead, against the run of play, but a wonder strike from Josh Ginnelly restored parity before the interval and an exquisite front-post finish from Shankland, ten minutes after the interval saw Hearts take all three points.

The Jambos were at Ibrox for their final away match of the season. They got off to the perfect start when Lawrence Shankland bundled the ball home from close range inside the opening minute.

From that point, it was all about game management and just when it looked like Hearts were going to head down the tunnel a goal to the good at half-time, an unfortunate slip from James Hill allowed Todd Cantwell the opportunity to equalise as he finished neatly past Zander Clark to level the scores with the final kick of the half.

Things didn't get much better for Hearts in the early exchanges of the second half as a Toby Sibbick error allowed in Fashion Sakala and

his effort had just enough on it to beat Zander Clark and complete the comeback for the home side.

Hearts kept chipping away and they found a late leveller in stoppage time as Garang Kuol bagged his first goal for the club in dramatic fashion.

Unfortunately, results elsewhere meant third place was now out of reach and Hearts would have to avoid defeat to their rivals on the final day at Tynecastle to secure fourth spot.

It had all the makings of a classic, nail-biting afternoon in Gorgie. Hibs had the chance to snatch fourth spot from right under Hearts' noses, despite spending the majority of the season below the Jambos in the league table.

Like all derbies, this one started at 100mph. Yutaro Oda opened the scoring with his first goal in maroon after just eight minutes and just when it looked like Hearts could give their neighbours another beating, the men in maroon were reduced to ten men.

In almost identical fashion to the Celtic match, Alex Cochrane was again shown a straight red card after a VAR review and Hearts would have to play the remaining hour with ten men.

Things got a whole lot tougher when Kevin Nisbet equalised from the resulting free-kick. Hibs now had an hour against ten men to find the winning goal that would see them finish above Hearts in the league.

The visitors huffed and puffed, and they came close from set plays, but Hearts stood firm and held on to ensure that despite the disappointment of missing out on third spot, Edinburgh stayed maroon.

SNAPS FROM A SEASON

Over the course of Season 2022/23: a pack of dedicated photographers followed Hearts up and down the country. From Perth to Paisley, Tynecastle to Tannadice, they documented another memorable season for the boys in maroon! Here are some of the best snaps...

Sibbick's Silence

Hearts defender Toby Sibbick lets the Hibs fans know what he thinks of them with this iconic derby day celebration! The Englishman scored the final goal in a thrilling 3-0 Scottish Cup triumph at Easter Road – running almost the full length of the pitch before cheekily lifting the ball over David Marshall.

Goal of the Season

Stephen Humphrys is mobbed by his Hearts team-mates after scoring from his own half against Dundee United. The Tannadice men were sent packing in a 3-1 victory, with Humphrys' rocket late in the game wrapping up all three points. The sensational strike would later be crowned as the SPFL's Goal of the Season.

Michie's Moment

Hearts Women midfielder Cailin Michie can't hide her delight after picking up a valuable point against Rangers at Oriam. The January 2023 stalemate with the Glasgow side was the first time the women in maroon had picked up a point against Rangers after turning semi-professional.

Wish You Were Ear

Pardon the pun…

Cammy and Cochers

Cammy Devlin and Alex Cochrane: football friends.

Shankland's Strike

No explanation required here!

Capital Cup Champions

Captain Georgia Hunter leads the celebrations after Hearts Women lift the Capital Cup at Tynecastle!

Roar of the Crowd

James Hill and Alex Cochrane drink in the adoration of the Wheatfield Stand after another Hearts win at Tynecastle

AIDAN DENHOLM
BACK TO BUSINESS

A penny for boyhood Jambo, Aidan Denholm's thoughts around 7:40PM in the Rosenborg tie. A first European start, in front of a packed house at Tynecastle. He sat down with Jamie McIntosh to reflect on what was a memorable night for the teenager.

"It certainly is something that I will remember for the rest of my life."

It's hardly a surprise to see the 19-year-old is still smiling away. And who can blame him.

It could have turned out so differently for Aidan Denholm, who was on his way out the door at Tynecastle until Frankie McAvoy and Steven Naismith joined the first team coaching staff.

For the second half of last season, Denholm struggled on loan at East Fife, after being told a new contract at Tynecastle would not be forthcoming.

In the first half of the season however, he had impressed in a Hearts B side having its debut season in the Lowland League under the guidance of Naismith.

Many of Denholm's attributes are in fact similar to that of Hearts' Technical Director. He has bags of energy and a clear enthusiasm for the game, which is crucial when you play in the middle of the park.

Comfortable in possession and never shy in raising his voice or diving into a tackle, Denholm was a key figure for the Wee Jambos last season.

But going from the likes of Central Park and Netherdale to starting European games under the lights at Tynecastle, is some turnaround. So, how did the midfielder keep his emotions in check in the hours leading up to the victory over Rosenborg?

"When you get told you are starting in a European game like that, you need to keep yourself calm," he explained.

"Credit to the boys in the changing room, they were talking me through it. Reminding me to play my game and remember what got me to this stage in the first place. Then just take it all in and enjoy it.

"I found out on matchday that I was starting. I texted my Mum and Dad straight away and then just tried to stay calm.

"You do get the butterflies, of course you do.

Especially, when that roar goes up seconds before kick-off. Being a Hearts fan myself, you dream of playing at Tynecastle on nights like that.

"I have never played in front of anything close to that. Credit to the fans. They stuck behind us, even when we conceded that early goal and that's a night I'll remember for the rest of my life."

There were a couple of nervy moments in the early stages for the youngster, but that is hardly surprising, and after 60 minutes, he left the field of play after putting in a great shift for the men in maroon.

Denholm's performance was an encouraging sign of the sort of talent that lurks in the Hearts Academy and one that can thrive from the experience gained in the Lowland League. However, it was Denholm's midfield partner that stole the show.

Two goals from Cammy Devlin sent Hearts through to the play-off round and while I'm sure Denholm would've loved to have found the net himself, he admitted he was delighted for the Aussie, who Denholm himself sees similarities to in his own game.

"I really ran myself into the ground, but I enjoyed every minute of it and obviously the most important thing was to get through to the next round.

"This is the best dressing room I've been in with regards to the boys helping me through a big game like that and keeping me focused. Losing that early goal obviously wasn't the best start, but we scored at crucial times, and I was so buzzing for Cammy.

"Playing alongside him makes my job so much easier as he is just like me, energetic and keen to get stuck in."

There are lot of aspects to this story that add to the narrative. Denholm could so easily have been pulling another side's jersey over his head and running out at another stadium to ply his trade.

Despite his age, he remains level-headed, admitting that the uncertainty surrounding new contracts is all part of a career in football. Nevertheless, Denholm remains at Tynecastle, and he is thankful to the coaching staff for trusting him.

"You have to respect the decision," he said. "It's part of football. I wasn't the only player that was told at that time that they would be leaving the club.

"I was on loan at East Fife at the time and because they are a part-time club, I was still at Oriam, and I just tried to keep going.

"I wasn't trying to prove anyone wrong. It was more just trying to prove to myself that when I got given chances like I did, that I can take them.

"That's a credit to Frankie, Naisy and Gordy for having the belief to start me in a game like that. I hope I repaid them.

"When I was told I was getting released, I still had a conversation with Naisy. It was mainly him just saying 'I'll try my best for you to get you other clubs. So, he was still doing his best for me even when I was going to be leaving.

"When I was away having trials at a few clubs down south, I saw Naisy was given the job on an interim basis. We had another conversation and he just told me that I had to believe in myself a bit more.

"I played under him with the B Team, so I knew the way he played and vice versa. Going into pre-season that was huge for me. I played in some of the friendlies, and I did okay, so it was just about showing it in training.

"For me, Naisy is the best coach I've had in terms of man-management. I can't speak highly enough of how he's been with me, both with the B Team, when I heard the news that I was going to be

released and now since I've been in with the first team.

"It's not just Naisy either. I have had plenty of conversations with Frankie last season as well when he was involved with the academy, and I know Gordy from last season too.

"The three of them bring very different things to the table and credit to all three of them for giving a 19 year-old a chance in one of the club's biggest games so far this season.

"It just shows that they are willing to give the young guys a chance if they do their graft and work hard and that there is a pathway from the B Team to the first team."

Finally, Denholm has received his fair share of praise from Hearts fans on social media, but he admits it's still early days and he is determined to maintain his performance levels and stay in and around the first team squad.

"I am on social media, and I have seen the praise I have been getting, but I don't really take too much notice of it, as nice as it is to read.

"It's only been a few games and I've set the standard now, which the fans will expect me to keep up, so that's down to me and me alone to maintain those standards."

2023/24 FIRST TEAM SQUAD

1

CRAIG GORDON

Country: Scotland

2

FRANKIE KENT

Country: England

3

STEPHEN KINGSLEY

Country: Scotland

4

CRAIG HALKETT

Country: Scotland

5

PETER HARING

Country: Austria

6

BENI BANINGIME

Country: DR Congo

7

JORGE GRANT

Country: England

8

CALEM NIEUWENHOF

Country: Australia

9

LAWRENCE SHANKLAND

Country: Scotland

10

LIAM BOYCE

Country: Northern Ireland

11

YUTARO ODA

Country: Japan

12

MICHAEL MCGOVERN

Country: Northern Ireland

13

NATHANIEL ATKINSON

Country: Australia

14

CAMMY DEVLIN

Country: Australia

15

KYE ROWLES

Country: Australia

16

ANDY HALLIDAY

Country: Scotland

17

ALAN FORREST

Country: Scotland

18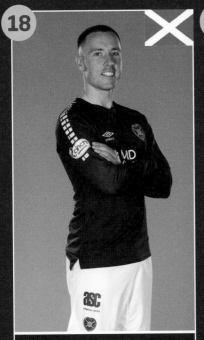

BARRIE McKAY

Country: Scotland

19

ALEX COCHRANE

Country: England

21

TOBY
SIBBICK

Country: England

22

AIDAN
DENHOLM

Country: Scotland

23

HARRY
STONE

Country: Scotland

25

FINLAY
POLLOCK

Country: Scotland

27

MACAULAY
TAIT

Country: Scotland

28

ZANDER CLARK

Country: Scotland

30

KYOSUKE TAGAWA

Country: Japan

51

ALEX LOWRY

Country: Scotland

77

KENNETH VARGAS

Country: Costa Rica

WORDSEARCH

Find the Hearts related words in the grid. Words can go horizontally, vertically and diagonally.

```
          M U S N E                               D E N E S
          T N Z P T F B                         C E Q Y K C I
        U V L A C O K U S I                   C J I J F X U O R J
      G S X B S S B O J O Y O               W H T P Q J H Y E T A X
      B Z X M F N K U R Q X F U            Q K F B S N F X M P S I E
    Z N R Q F K W J S F Z U H H L M A Y V H B H Y Y F A D M Q H
    A R U A H A Y U Q T P L V Q P C H K T H Z R A S X E P R L N
    N G V K E O X F U X Z X P W I B F P N K M U D N O Y R Z I D
    D Q H S A N E C M W U O T Y N E C A S T L E E T K I S H Z Z
    E B M E R O A A N P H H U M D P W Q F Z S J J Y U L L M A D
    R C L O K C R B E H L U M A X I B K I T I J O C K H A I J B
    G W F Z F A Y T J U V P G S D F A X T C B W A U U J F N T M
    E N H M Z N H I R A K G A W L T N R P Y B G C O T I Y S D R
    G H Z P V G R W J K T G O R G I E X U I F W A O O L C K
    Z T L W J X F J P I S X M J U N T Y T C X A Y J F S I X
      A L D W O H T B M G V P H I G Y R A K C W X R Q J F
      Y T I R Z K H C T Q R Q Z I Q E R I R K O T F H
      R D V M I A Y L F X R H M D A O Z B G D E H
        D E V L I N R U G S H E T G N T Z T N R
        X R L T X E Q W F B X V A E C J H M
        U N J J X R X T B S J Y I L X L
          W P D F A A U P O I A H W X
          R U S Z R S L O D H T A
          I C O W F K O X N V
            T U S F Z O R I
            I B Z R V U
            J Z C P
            C F
```

TYNECASTLE   **ZANDER**   **YUTARO**

BANINGIME   **HMFC**   **JOCK**

SHANKLAND   **GORGIE**

DEVLIN   **SIBBICK**

ANSWERS ON PAGES 60-61

SPOT THE BALL

Can you spot which is the real ball in the photos below?.

ANSWERS ON PAGES 60-61

MISFITS

ANSWERS ON PAGES 60-61

Can you figure out which parts of the mixed-up faces belongs to the corresponding Hearts player?

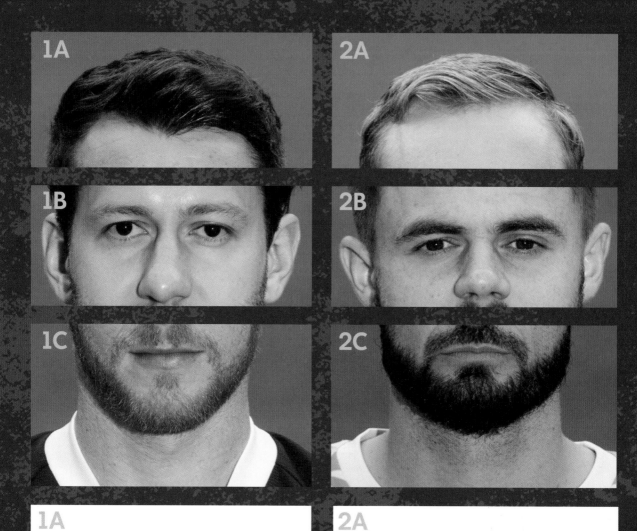

1A _____

1B _____

1C _____

2A _____

2B _____

2C _____

THE HEARTS QUIZ

1. Alan Forrest scored Hearts' first league goal of the season against Ross County. Which Scottish Premiership club did he play for the season before joining the Jambos?

2. Lawrence Shankland was Hearts' top goalscorer in season 22/23, but who was second?

3. Stephen Humphrys won the goal of the season at the Hearts Player of the Year awards, but who did he score his wonder goal against?

4. Who kept more clean sheets in season 22/23? Was it:

   ☐ A) Craig Gordon

   ☐ B) Zander Clark

5. Hearts Women achieved their highest-ever league finish in season 22/23, but where exactly did they finish?

6. Which team did Hearts score the most goals against in a league match last season?

   ☐ A) Aberdeen

   ☐ B) Ross County

7. Hearts' European journey for season 22/23 ended in Istanbul against Basaksehir. Who scored Hearts' only goal that night?

8. January 2023 saw Hearts record back-to-back 3-0 victories over Hibernian with four different goalscorers. How many can you name?

9. Who scored Hearts' first goal under manager Steven Naismith? Was it:

   ☐ A) Alex Cochrane

   ☐ B) Cammy Devlin

10. Which Hearts player scored a last-minute penalty against St Mirren in a 2-2 draw in May?

ANSWERS ON PAGES 60-61

THE KEYS TO HEARTS WOMEN'S SUCCESS

Season 22/23 was one to remember for Hearts Women. With their highest-ever finish in SWPL1, a new brand of high-press attacking football, and international stars signing for the club, this really has been the coming-of-age season for Hearts Women.

The appointment of Spanish manager Eva Olid was always going to be a long-term project, but the results this season have been so good that it has turned out to be a short-term project.

The pre-season objective for this Hearts side, which had received an increased budget and had recruited in large numbers was a top-six finish. It has to be said that without taking anything away from the team, who worked very hard to achieve that, they did so with relative ease.

So, let's take a look at the key players in this squad and how Hearts achieved so much last season.

Goalkeeper

Charlotte Parker-Smith has enjoyed another brilliant season in goals for Hearts. She remains one of, if not the best shot-stoppers in the league, however, she hasn't been as busy as in previous seasons and that is because of the improved defensive unit in front of her.

Defence

Hearts have flipped between a defensive four and five throughout the season, initially starting the season with a five, Olid opted for the back four for the second-half of the season and Hearts have remained a very solid defensive unit. Skipper Georgia Hunter is continuing to develop since progressing through the club's youth academy and alongside her, is Jamaican internationalist, Vyan Sampson, both are very solid central defenders and are good both in the air and with the ball at their feet.

At full-back, Hearts have opted largely for Emma Brownlie on the right and Addie Handley on the left, the former, who signed from Rangers in the summer of 2022, brings with her plenty of experience having lifted the SWPL title with the Gers the previous season. Handley is the opposite, a young inexperienced defender, who after working her way into the side at the beginning of the year, hasn't looked back. Addie still has a lot to learn, but she is progressing very well and is starting to receive the recognition she deserves, after receiving call-ups to represent Scotland Under-19s.

Midfield

In Midfield, Hearts have a mixture of experience and quality. Let's start with the Player of the Year for the 22/23 campaign, Ciara Grant. Another player Hearts picked up from Rangers, Grant brings real steel to the Hearts midfield. She is comfortable in possession and very rarely does she give the ball away. She is box-to-box but is also extremely accurate from the dead-ball, with her corners and free-kicks usually bang on the money. Not to mention her perfect penalty at Easter Road against Hibernian.

Alongside Ciara, in what is usually a midfield three is Monica Forsyth. After suffering cruciate ligament damage in December 2021, Monica, who won the Rising Star Award at the Player of the Year awards, spent 12 months on the sidelines, before returning to the pitch hungrier than ever to succeed. She has been like a new signing for Hearts and is often tasked with being the creative player in the midfield three. Confident and comfortable in possession, Monica is also, a strong and willing runner, giving her all the attributes to be a top-quality midfield player.

As for the third midfield player, Hearts had options. Cailin Michie featured regularly at the start of the season, but then the likes of Aimee Anderson, Rebecca McAllister and Erin Rennie provided some competition for places. It was an area of the pitch Hearts were strong in throughout the season.

Attack

Again, this was an area where Hearts were spoilt for choice. Georgia Timms was banging the goals in at the start of the season and was flanked by the likes of Katie Rood, Gwen Davies, or Jenny Smith, who were all very direct and keen to put crosses into the box, with great success too.

In truth, Hearts probably haven't scored as many goals as they should have considering the number of chances they created on average in each match, but nevertheless, the pace and power of Timms in particular, was a problem for every backline in the country.

The manager

Eva Olid has installed a new belief at Hearts Women. There is definitely a winning mentality and a will to succeed at the club now and that ultimately comes from the manager.

It's hardly surprising that Olid's managerial style has similarities to the football she grew up watching in Barcelona. She likes her sides to dominate the ball, be aggressive and look to go forward. Out of possession, it is all about pressing and winning the ball back.

The final word

The 2022/23 campaign will be remembered as the season when Hearts Women established themselves as one of the top women's teams in the country. A lot of hard work had been put in over the years to lay the groundwork for Eva Olid to come in and take this team to the next level and with such a talented crop of young girls throughout the academy, Hearts Women will no doubt be a wonderful place for young girls to come and play the beautiful game for years to come.

The Heart and Soul of Edinburgh

FOUNDED
1874

LEAGUE CHAMPIONS
1895, 1897, 1958, 1960

SCOTTISH CUP WINNERS
1891, 1896, 1901, 1906,
1956, 1998, 2006, 2012

LEAGUE CUP WINNERS
1954/55, 1958/59,
1959/60, 1962/63

MOST LEAGUE APPEARANCES
Gary Mackay
515 (1980-1997)

MOST LEAGUE GOALS
John Robertson
214 (1983-1998)

Q&A

FINLAY POLLOCK

As a kid, did you always want to be a footballer?
"Definitely. Being young, every single day at school you used to be out playing football on the Astro, you never wanted to be in class, you just always wanted to be out playing, so yeah that was all I really wanted to do."

Did you play school/club football before Hearts?
"I played both school and club football. I played school football for Stewart's Melville, but I also played for Spartans which was my local team. I was playing for Hearts while I was still at Spartans before that pro-youth side of it began.

"I think I was around 8 when I first started playing for Hearts and then I signed the pro-youth contract at the age of 10."

How old were you when you really thought you could 'make it'?
"Ever since I joined Spartans really. It was just always something that I loved doing after school. I always looked forward to playing. At first, I was just enjoying it, but then I realised it was something I wanted to pursue for the rest of my life.

"So, I'm just fortunate that I was able to work hard as a young kid at Spartans to eventually get noticed by a club like Hearts."

What was it like to sign pro-youth?
"I was actually told by Hibs first that they were going to offer me a pro-youth contract, as I was at both Hibs and Hearts at the time. I told Hibs no at first, because being a Hearts fan, I was hoping to be offered a contract by Hearts. So, I took that gamble that Hearts would offer me a contract and thankfully they did.

"I was delighted with that. I was so happy. That meant I left Spartans and focused solely on Hearts and when you're that age, putting on the strip and playing against other pro-youth teams was just a dream come true."

Your favourite moment at Hearts so far?
"My debut was amazing. That final day of the Championship season at Tynecastle was brilliant. Getting to spend time with my family on the pitch. Also, being a part of the European campaign was amazing.

"The debut was weird because obviously there were no fans there. I remember I was supposed to make my debut the week before, but I had a thigh injury, so I had rehab for a week and was just desperately trying to get back fit."

"I was on the bench, and we scored early goals that day, so I was wondering if I would get on or not, but then the manager told me to warm up so my heart rate went pretty high.

"My Dad managed to get in the crowd as well which was brilliant, so just to make my debut under those circumstances, with us lifting the trophy, and getting a medal and getting to keep it. That is something I'll remember for the rest of my life."

Most nervous you've been in your career?
"That debut was up there. I was pretty nervous when I was starting in the Premier Sports Cup, but I was able to get rid of them quicker because I was starting, but being on the bench for that Inverness game was a long wait. I was very nervous that day, but that shows you care."

Finlay's top tips for young players
1. One of the big things is try and train how you play. That is a phrase used by a lot of people, but it just makes you better prepared for games. You'll have more match sharpness and in yourself, you'll feel readier which will increase your confidence.

2. Recovery: I have struggled a lot through injuries. We get much better recovery now, but when you're younger, you just go home, have a shower and play Xbox. That means you stiffen up, so one thing I'd really recommend to young people is to stretch off. That makes a massive impact.

3. Nutrition: That makes a massive impact before and after a game. We've been told that the number of calories we burn is probably more than we take in. We get meetings at Hearts now about what stuff is good to take before games, things with lots of carbohydrates, but also the timing of when you take it is very important also, so you get the maximum benefit. Normally between 1-2 hours after the game is ideal and that will help maximise recovery and reduce the risk of injury.

Finlay's Favourite meals
"Before games, I cook some noodles and veg. But with the first team, you get a pre-match meal and you're basically given a selection to choose from. This includes eggs on toast, jam on toast, pasta or chicken dishes. That's all my favourite stuff to have before.

"As for afterwards, chicken strips, chicken burgers, and Yazoo milkshakes are good for after, but even hydration tablets to mix with water to make sure you are staying hydrated are great."

Finlay is here to stay
"I was buzzing when I was offered it. I just had all my eyes on that and couldn't wait to sign it and stay here. I've supported them since I was a little boy. It was always the team I wanted to play for, so hopefully this year I can get more of a chance in the first team to cement my place and play for the team I love."

HIS NAME IS
DREW BUSBY

Hearts legend Drew Busby sadly passed away in July 2022, aged 74. We take a look back at his footballing career with a special focus on his time in the famous maroon jersey.

Drew was born in Glasgow in December 1947 and had spells with Dumbarton United, Third Lanark, Partick Thistle, Vale of Leven, and Airdrieonians before signing for Hearts in May 1973.

He will be remembered fondly by supporters of all the clubs he represented during his playing career and will always have his place in history after scoring Third Lanark's final goal before the club's demise in April 1967.

The Jambos paid what at the time, was a club record fee of £35,000 to secure the services of Busby from Airdrieonians.

A versatile attacker, Drew could play as a striker or in a more offensive midfield role. He quickly became a fans' favourite at Tynecastle due to not only his talent, which was evident from an early stage of his time in Gorgie, but also his work-rate.

Busby made 277 appearances in total for Hearts and scored 90 goals, many of which were memorable strikes.

During six years at the club between 1973 and 1979, Busby provided Hearts fans with many memorable moments in what were tough times for the football club.

Perhaps one of Drew's more memorable goals in maroon came in the European Cup Winners Cup victory in a 5-1 against Lokomotiv Leipzig in September 1976.

Nicknamed 'Buzz Bomb', Drew departed Hearts in 1979, with the 31 year-old joining Toronto Blizzard, in Canada, where he spent two seasons.

Drew returned to finish his career in Scotland following his time across the pond. He went on to play for Greenock Morton, before joining Queen of the South as player-manager.

Some of Drew's final moments in the beautiful game saw him carry out some scouting for St Mirren before he joined the pub game and opened a pub in Dumbarton called The Waverley.

Drew was unsurprisingly inducted into the Hearts Hall of Fame in 2018.

When the news broke of Drew's passing, Hearts fans, among many others were quick to pay tribute to a player many would regard as one of the best they saw in maroon.

A match at Tynecastle saw supporters pay a collective tribute to Buzz Bomb. A TIFO display that read BUSBY 8, the number which he wore for the Jambos, spread across the whole of the Wheatfield Stand, highlighted just how much of a club legend Drew really was.

Whereas his former team-mate at Morton, Roy Baines described Drew as: "Hard as nails on and off the pitch yet a quiet, lovely guy. Drew could sort out the dirtiest of players in the opposition. And sort out any idiots in the dressing room."

Club Historian David Speed wrote a profile for Drew's induction to the Hall of Fame, some of the passages read as follows:

"Drew Busby was immensely popular in a maroon shirt, because he was always fully committed to Hearts and possessed a truly remarkable work-rate. Drew could also use the ball to advantage and his shooting was legendary, earning him 90 goals in 277 appearances (84 of these in 256 competitive matches), with many scored in spectacular fashion.

"Hearts brought Drew Busby to Tynecastle in May 1973 for a club record fee of £35,000. The uncompromising attacker gave nothing less than 100% over the next six years, during which time he helped Hearts to qualify for the initial Premier Division. Indeed, Drew scored the club's first goal in this competition, at Dens Park, Dundee, in September 1975. He also played in the Scottish Cup Final in 1976 against Rangers which was immediately followed by the club's round-the-world tour.

"Drew was a key member of the squad that took part in the European Cup Winners Cup the following season. He scored in the unforgettable home victory over Lokomotive Leipzig and also netted in the next round against Hamburger SV. Another highlight came in the Texaco Cup, away to Everton in September 1973, when he scored the only goal of the game. He also made Semi-Final appearances in both the League Cup and the Scottish Cup and, in addition, Drew played in Hearts' Centenary celebration game in August 1974 against Tottenham Hotspur.

"After Hearts' shock relegation in 1976-77, Drew was a prominent of the team that immediately won promotion. On the way back to the Premier Division, on Christmas Eve 1977, both he and Willie Gibson famously scored a hat-trick in Hearts' 7-0 win at Arbroath and secured the sponsor's prize of a crate of whisky for every hat-trick scored. Unfortunately, Hearts went down again in 1979 and at the age of 31, Drew moved to Toronto Blizzard in May that year.

"Hearts suffered a number of hammer-blows during the mid-seventies, but Drew Busby was a light at the end of the tunnel, and he always made it worthwhile coming along to Tynecastle, despite the set-backs.

"After two seasons in Canada, the dynamic 5'8" attacker played for Greenock Morton and became player-manager of Queen of the South. Drew then did some scouting for St Mirren before moving into the licensed trade where he ran The Waverley in Dumbarton.

"Before recent renovations, a giant poster of Drew Busby sat on a floodlight pylon after supporters voted him one of their fourteen favourite players.

"Drew will forever have his place in Gorgie Folklore".

R.I.P. Drew

WE TIED OUR SCARVES, AROUND THE FUNNEL...

Season 2022/23 saw Heart of Midlothian make a thrilling return to European action! This was the club's first European adventure since 2016, and our first outing in the Group Stages of a UEFA competition since 2004, which had Hearts supporters everywhere laying out their passports with glee! Take a look below to see where the Hearts jetted off to around the continent on a European tour.

📍 FIRST STOP: ST. GALLEN

SWITZERLAND VS FC ZÜRICH, AUGUST 2022

When the Jambos stepped onto the tarmac at Edinburgh Airport that summer, it was Eastern Switzerland that was to be the first step on Hearts' journey around the continent. The boys in maroon, thanks to the previous season's exploits, had earned themselves a spot in the play-off round of the UEFA Europa League.

There were some formidable teams in the mix but after the draw was conducted at UEFA Headquarters in Nyon, Hearts' name was pulled out of the hat alongside the champions of Switzerland: FC Zürich.

Curiously the first leg of the tie wasn't actually played in the Swiss capital – but an hour away at Kybunpark, the home of FC St. Gallen. This was because there was a concert on at Zürich's home ground: Letzigrund.

Thousands of Jambos made the trip over, enjoying the charms of St. Gallen's cobbled streets that were not unlike Edinburgh, and watched as Lawrence Shankland scored a 22nd minute penalty to catapult Hearts into the lead.

Zürich hit back with two goals before half-time, with the game finishing 2-1. Hearts were eventually defeated 1-0 in the second leg at Tynecastle, bowing out of the play-offs, but a memorable journey and spirited home leg performance gave the maroon faithful something to cheer about.

NEXT UP: RIGA

LATVIA VS RFS, SEPTEMBER 2022

Hearts picked up a vital away victory in the Latvian capital to get their UEFA Europa Conference League campaign off the ground. The Jambos arrived at the Skonto Stadium in high hopes, and were soon rewarded.

Goals from Lawrence Shankland and Alan Forrest secured a massive 2-0 victory over the Latvian side, with players and fans coming together at full-time for a rowdy celebration. Riga was a charming city, full of things to see, and the travelling maroon contingent had an excellent time.

THIRD STOP: FLORENCE

ITALY VS FIORENTINA, OCTOBER 2022

Despite Stephen Humphrys' early goal against the Italian giants, Il Viola roared back and secured a comfortable 5-1 victory. That said, the Florentines proved to be eventual Conference League finalists – so perhaps there's some comfort to draw on there!

This trip was, for many Hearts supporters, the highlight of the group stage adventures. The Italian city was dripping in spectacular vistas and immense history. Jambos from near and far flocked to areas outside the great cathedrals: the Duomo and Santa Maria Novella.

Friends and family walked around the ancient streets in awe and, with fine weather complementing the entire experience, it was truly a once-in-a-lifetime experience for many and particularly those who may have been on their first European trip with Hearts.

Of course, it would be remiss not to mention the away end at the Artemio Franchi Stadium. Teeming with Hearts fans, a sea of maroon that met the gilded art deco, purple surroundings, the scenes of celebration at the early goal from Humphrys was sheer bedlam. An explosion of joy that was a wonderful sight to behold.

Hearts supporters did their club and country proud, displaying immaculate behaviour on their visit to the Tuscan city.

END OF THE ROAD: ISTANBUL

TURKEY VS BASAKSEHIR, NOVEMBER 2022

Hearts bowed out of Group A of the Conference League with one last hurrah: a trip to the Turkish capital of Istanbul, the crossroads of the world, for a matchup with Istanbul Basaksehir. One of the top sides in Turkey: they had former Premier League talents such as Mesut Özil and Nacer Chadli on the books – as well as exceptional footballers like Stefano Okaka and Bertrand Traoré.

In a mostly empty Fatih Terim Stadium, with the exception of a noisy contingent of Hearts supporters in the corner, the Turkish side were superior on the ball and walked away with a 3-1 victory; Nathaniel Atkinson scoring right at the end courtesy of a lovely assist in the build up from impressive youngster Finlay Pollock.

It was the last stop of the journey before Hearts gathered their things and returned to Scotland. A wonderful experience that whetted the appetite for even more journeys across the continent in the future.

We've travelled far, by bus and car...

CELEBRATING 150 YEARS

This season, Hearts' Chair, Ann Budge and the Chair of the Foundation of Hearts, Gerry Mallon unveiled the first marker of the Club's impending sesquicentennial season. The new gate at Gerards Yard features for the first time – a specially designed emblem marking 150 Years since Hearts' inception. Manufactured locally by Club Partner, Hepburn Fabrications, the gate is formed of solid steel with the beautiful new emblem forged in aluminium.

Celebrations of Hearts 150th anniversary will commence towards the start of Season 23-24 and will feature a range of events and initiatives that will involve the broadest possible cross section of supporters, families and the wider community. So, what can fans expect? Events will include:

· Pre-season friendlies
· a festival of family fun and football at Tynecastle
· a series of 'Evening With' events featuring club legends across the years and
· special gala dinners.

Hogmanay 2023 will be celebrated in style with dinners in both the Skyline and the Gorgie Suite and there will be special celebrations as we welcome in 2024 and reach the official anniversary date. Our first home game in January will see us hoist the Sesquicentennial Flag above the stadium.

Throughout the year, we will celebrate not just the well-known stories, but we will also provide an insight into hitherto unexplored moments in history. Our recent "Transcribathon" that saw a mini army of volunteers transform handwritten extracts from Club

Minutes Books from 1874 onwards into digital and searchable documents, has unearthed fascinating insights into key moments across the decades. These will be shared with supporters and we look forward to engaging with local schools to bring this rich heritage to life.

In addition to all the above, our friends from Two Halves Productions will stage A War of Two Halves for a final run in November 2024, as well as producing two exciting new historic shows for Fringe 2023 and Fringe 2024.

In anticipation of the 150th Anniversary, the Club and the Foundation of Hearts have been working on plans to enhance the Memorial at Haymarket in time for this year's Remembrance service. On top of that, we are in advanced discussions on the creation of a Maroon Mile which will run from the monument and Tynecastle Park.

All of the above will be special, but we have so much more planned.

Ann Budge commented:

"We all know that some 10 years ago, there was a real danger that Hearts would not have reached this magnificent milestone. The incredible backing of supporters and the Foundation of Hearts changed history and now, as the largest fan-owned club in the UK, we will celebrate 150 years as a Scottish football icon, safe in the knowledge that the future of the club has been secured for future generations to come."

Gerry Mallon, Chair of the Foundation of Hearts commented:

"Without Ann Budge and the amazing fans of Heart of Midlothian, it's very doubtful if our club would have had the privilege of celebrating its 140th, let alone its 150th, anniversary. What a story this has been and what a moment we have reached together. A milestone like this must be properly celebrated and the programme which the club has so expertly drawn up will give all of us the opportunity both to reflect on our rich history and to enjoy our present – made all the more special by the enormous challenges we have faced and overcome. Everyone involved with the Foundation can stand tall today and rightly be proud that the legacy of those 150 years has been upheld and can be passed on to new generations. It's very fitting that the first celebration focuses on these gates, a great metaphor for throwing open the story of our club and ushering in a bright, positive future."

THE 150TH ANNIVERSARY KIT

Heart of Midlothian Football Club is proud to unveil the stunning new 2023/24 Umbro third kit. Celebrating the club's identity as we look towards its 150th anniversary, the new third kit is inspired by Hearts' very first kit from 1874.

Featuring textured pique fabric, this kit brings 'old school' to life with a particular focus on the oversized club crest, mirroring that inaugural kit from two centuries ago. Completing the iconic kit are white shorts with maroon flashes, and socks with maroon and white circular bands.

Time Capsule
1957-8 LEAGUE CHAMPIONS

In 2024, we celebrate the 150th anniversary of the founding of Heart of Midlothian Football Club. Over the course of the next two seasons, spanning the course of those celebrations, we'll reflect on the greatest moments and achievements in the club's history. Hearts historian and collector Gary Cowen reflects on our Championship winning team of 1957-58…

We're going to start by looking at perhaps our greatest league season of all, the 1957-8 league championship.

Hearts had won the League Cup in 1954 and the Scottish Cup in 1956 but Tommy Walker's men had always fallen just short over a 34-game season, finishing second in 1954 and 1957 and despite having the league's top scorer in 1950, 1954, 1955 and 1956. Hibs' golden age at the start of the 1950's had fizzled out and Kilmarnock's was yet to arrive. Celtic were not the force they are today and Hearts' main challengers were Aberdeen and, inevitably, Rangers.

But from the off in 1957-8, it was clear that Hearts meant business with an attack which was almost impossible to stop, a miserly defence and a midfield controlled by perhaps the best half backs ever to play in maroon, John Cumming and Dave Mackay, ably supported by George Thomson and Andy Bowman. Whilst the 'Terrible Trio' of Conn, Bauld and Wardhaugh were all still at the club, form and

injury kept the first two out of the side for most of the season. Alex Young and Jimmy Murray, who went to the World Cup in Sweden with Scotland at the end of the season, were exceptionally able deputies.

The first two matches, a 6-0 win against Dundee and a 7-2 away win at Airdrie were emphatic but could Hearts keep up that sort of form against the rather more difficult proposition of Hibs in an Edinburgh derby? Our rivals were duly dispatched 3-1 and when Hearts hit nine against East Fife and followed that up with wins against Aberdeen and, more importantly, Rangers, the club started to be mentioned as potential champions. The home win over Aberdeen as the team won 4-0 was as impressive as a 3-2 success at Ibrox against the previous season's champions Rangers with Bauld and Wardhaugh on target for Hearts.

At that stage, Hearts were top of the league, a point ahead of surprise packages Raith Rovers who had also only lost once and six and ten points respectively ahead of Celtic and Rangers, each of whom had played four games less.

Any thoughts, however, that the Hearts bubble might have burst with the loss at Shawfield were firmly put to bed in the next match at Tynecastle as the Hearts forward line exploded into life, scoring nine against Falkirk with Alex Young on target four times and Dave Mackay a 'mere' three. That win was the catalyst for an astonishing run of fifteen wins in a row for Hearts as they pulled further away from the chasing pack behind them in the league. Ten goals were scored in the next three games before Christmas and as Hearts fans sat down to Christmas lunch, Hearts were five points clear of Hibs and nine ahead of Celtic who still had four games in hand. The destiny of the title was now in Hearts' own hands.

A hugely important festive period saw Hearts record 2-0 wins over their nearest challengers at Celtic Park and Easter Road and suddenly, Hearts were hot favourites to secure their first title since 1897 and led by nine points from Hibs, with Celtic now replaced by Rangers as Hearts' most likely challengers. But there was no let up from clinical Hearts who scored 23 goals in their next five league games including rattling seven past Third Lanark, against whom we'd dropped a point earlier in the season.

As early as February 1958, Hearts celebrated their 100th league goal of the season, Alfie Conn scoring Hearts' fourth against Motherwell at Fir Park to bring up the century of goals. By the time we reached March 1958, it was very much Hearts' title to lose. Going into the match against Celtic at Tynecastle, we were a massive sixteen points ahead of Rangers though they had five games in hand. Even if they won all of those games, we'd still have a six point cushion at the top. The Celtic game showed Hearts at their magnificent best, scoring twice in the first seven minutes and winning the game 5-3.

Hearts eventually clinched the title after an exciting 3-2 win at Love Street against St Mirren on 12 April 1958. By this time, Hearts had secured 56 points of a possible 62 and with ten games still to play, the best Rangers could hope for was 57 points from ten wins. When Alex Young scored the winning goal with seventeen minutes of the game left, Hearts had 58 points and an unassailable lead in the title race meaning a third League title for Hearts and their most emphatic success to date.

Gary Cowen

The Board of Directors, Manager, Players, Trainers and Staff of The Heart of Midlothian Football Club desire to express their appreciation of the kind congratulations which have been so warmly extended to them on the occasion of their winning the Scottish League Championship. This achievement has been made possible by the loyal support and constant encouragement of their many friends.

TYNECASTLE PARK
EDINBURGH

April 1958

THE STATISTICS

Hearts scored 132 league goals and conceded just 29, giving a goal difference of over 100 goals.

Three Hearts forwards scored 20 league goals in the season: Jimmy Wardhaugh scored 28, followed closely by Jimmy Murray with 27, and Alex Young who scored 24.

These days, of course, it is much harder for a team outwith the big two to enjoy league success. But at the first home league game of the season, we can dream about a team like the best ever Hearts team – the team of 1957-8.

Cult Heroes
1998 SQUAD

"And the long, long, wait is over! Hearts have won the Scottish Cup!"

An iconic piece of commentary that will still give many Hearts fans, young or old, goosebumps to this day. It was Hearts' first piece of silverware in 36 years and for those in the squad that day, instant legendary status in Gorgie was achieved.

It's what will define many players' time at a certain club. Trophies. Everybody wants to win them and ultimately that can make or break how not only fans remember certain players, but also how players reflect on their time at certain clubs.

We are of course talking about the Hearts side that defeated Rangers 2-1 to win the 1998 Scottish Cup in the glorious sunshine at Celtic Park, thanks to goals from Colin Cameron and Stephane Adam

Looking back on the day itself, the first thing that stands out is some of the names in the opposition ranks. Sergio Porrini, Lorenzo Amoruso, Gennaro Gattuso, and Brian Laudrup were just some of the European stars Rangers had in their ranks.

This is before you add the Scottish talent of Ally McCoist, Richard Gough, Ian Ferguson, Stuart McCall, and Gordon Durie.

As for Hearts, they had seven Scots in their starting line-up. An all-Scottish defence of Paul Ritchie, David McPherson, David Weir, and Gary Naysmith.

Colin Cameron, Steve Fulton, and Neil McCann in a five-man midfield alongside the late great, Stefano Salvatori and Austrian winger Thomas Flögel, which left Frenchman Stéphane Adam to lead the line, and oh boy, did he do just that.

It's interesting reading manager Jim Jefferies, another Hearts legend, words after the match. Rangers were a top team in the late 90s and although they weren't the only side to have suffered this, Rangers had recently beaten Hearts on numerous big occasions.

Jefferies' mindset was to always go out and try to win the game, like any manager, however on this occasion, he opted to be a little more defensive and set up to frustrate Rangers.

"Our tactics were spot-on," he said. "We had lost 13 goals to Rangers this season, so we decided to let them try to break us down. We gave them a problem but after McCoist scored it was the longest 10 minutes of my life."

Often in these situations, you need something to hang on to, as the likelihood is these top sides will eventually score, as all it takes is one mistake or moment of quality.

Hearts' game plan got off to the perfect start when they were awarded a penalty in the opening minute. Steve (Baggio) Fulton was incredibly fired up and even after Willie Young pointed to the penalty spot after Fulton had been brought down by Ian Ferguson, he still looked like he was filled with rage.

TENNENTS SCOTTISH CUP WINNERS 1997/98

Colin (Mickey) Cameron stepped up and sent Andy Goram the wrong way to give Hearts the dream start. From that point onwards, it was all about hanging on for Hearts, and that is something they would have worked on all week in training. Being disciplined without the ball, well-organised, and well-drilled in their shape when Rangers were in possession.

Hearts could almost touch the trophy when Amoruso's mistake let in Adam, whose volley had too much power for Goram, resulting in Hearts going two up, seven minutes into the second half.

McCoist came off the bench to halve the deficit in his last game for the club, nine minutes from time to set up a nervous ending.

Those who were there will recall the final moments, or maybe you won't depending on your pre-match routine, but after what felt like six months' worth of stoppage time, the final whistle sounded, and the celebrations could begin.

It is hard to choose which celebrations were more joyous, those in the stands, those on the pitch, or those that followed at Tynecastle, as thousands lined the Gorgie streets to welcome back the players and staff. Both had suffered so much heartache in recent years and all of that hurt and emotion was let out when Willie Young blew his whistle for the final time that afternoon.

Upon taking a closer look at those involved that afternoon, in Rousset, Hearts had an experienced veteran stopper who had enjoyed spells with Lyon, Rennes, Marseille, and Sochaux-Montbéliard before arriving in Edinburgh.

In the backline, Hearts had a mixture of experience and youth, McPherson was 34 at the time and provided some much-needed experience alongside David Weir, to Hearts' two young full-backs, Gary Naysmith and Paul Ritchie, who were aged 19 and 22 at the time.

In midfield, Salvatori just oozed class and again provided some vital experience alongside Cameron and Fulton. On the wing, McCann had previous experience for turning up and terrorising Rangers, and on the opposite flank Flogel again, was a very classy player.

Up top, Adam knew, as is often the case against the Old Firm, the opposition striker will need to work hard and is likely to feed off scraps. But, when his chance came along he made sure he took it, doubling Hearts' advantage with what turned out to be the winning goal.

As for those in the dugout, you will probably struggle to find two guys not only more genuine but more deserving than Jefferies and his assistant, Billy Brown. Both had suffered their fair share of cup final heartache at the club, but I am sure they will both say that '98 was worth the wait.

Finally, it's impossible to discuss '98 without mentioning firstly, club captain, Gary Locke, who was out injured at the time, and secondly, John Robertson, who was an unused sub in what would be his last game as a Hearts player.

Two fantastic servants to the maroon jersey down the years, both on and off the pitch, and like the rest of the '98 squad, they can be summed up in one word. Legends.

It's hard to believe it's been almost four years since Liam Boyce made his Hearts debut, on the 26th of January 2020, in a 2-1 victory over Rangers at Tynecastle.

It wasn't a great season for the Jambos, who ended up being demoted following the premature ending of the football season due to the Covid-19 pandemic, but that day was a very special afternoon at Tynecastle.

The men in maroon were good value for their win that afternoon and although they fell behind shortly after half-time, two familiar faces helped to turn the match on its head.

The equaliser arrived from the right boot of Steven Naismith. Craig Halkett pressured Glen Kamara into a mistake and the ball was prodded into the path of Boyce. He looked up and pulled the ball back for Naismith, who swept the ball over Allan McGregor and into the top corner.

Tynecastle was rocking by this point and the home fans sensed a winner. Connor Washington almost provided it, but his volley was cleared off the line.

Not to worry though, as seven minutes from time, Boyce popped up with a memorable winner.

Oliver Bozanic's cross from the left, found its way to Boyce at the back post. He jinked it back inside Joe Aribo and his left-foot shot took a deflection off Borna Barisic, completely deceiving McGregor in the Rangers goal.

Boyce wheeled away in celebration with a knee-slide in front of the Wheatfield Stand. The perfect way to introduce yourself to the Gorgie faithful.

"It was a quick couple of days if I remember rightly," said Boyce, remembering the match.

"I don't think I'd trained, and I wasn't sure if I was going to be playing or not but then I obviously started.

"I set up Naisy for the first goal as well which is funny. It was a great start to my Hearts career. The atmosphere that day was unbelievable and as a striker starting with a goal is what everyone wants to do."

Boyce missed much of the 2022/23 season through injury and slowly came back into the side at the start of the 23/24 campaign.

Watching on from the side-lines is never easy and it's been no different for Boycey. The Northern Irishman believes the key for any young player experiencing time on the treatment table is to maintain your social life in order to keep spirits high.

"When you have those wee calf injuries and you're out for short periods. Those ones can almost be harder and believe it or not, when you're out for nine months it's actually a bit easier in some respects.

"For me last season, it was probably only the group stage games in Europe that were hard to watch as they were the first couple of games. After that you just sort of forget about football and just focus on doing weights and gym work for nine months.

"So those shorter ones when you're close to being back, you can get a little impatient but when you're out for a long time it's a bit easier to put it to the back of your mind.

"For us players, football is your whole life. So, it's always important to have something in your life in the background. Obviously for me, that is my family and my kids. That's who makes me happy.

"But when I was younger and when I was playing in Germany, I would see friends and play FIFA, basically just have a social life.

"Make sure you don't have your whole life revolving around football as it puts too much pressure on you and takes the enjoyment out of it by making it more like a job.

It's impossible to speak with Boycey and not ask him about the Covid Scottish Cup semi-final against Hibernian at Hampden Park.

The tragic news of the passing of 2012 Scottish Cup winning captain Marius Zaliukas began to circle on social media during the first half.

Goals from Craig Wighton and Christian Doidge, saw the scores level as the game entered extra time. Kevin Nisbet squandered a huge opportunity to put Hibs ahead from the penalty spot as Craig Gordon denied him, before Aidy White won a penalty for the Jambos up the other end.

Up stepped Boyce and you know the rest. A goal that will have meant so much to so many people, for many different reasons. Lockdown was a tough time for every football fan, but there won't have been one Hearts fan that didn't think big Zal played a part that night.

"So, make sure you have things that can take your mind off football as that then makes it more enjoyable when you play."

It's hardly a surprise to hear that Boycey's top tip for any young players out there, who are dreaming of being footballers when they are older, is to practise, whenever and wherever you can.

"Everyone loves football," he said. "I think it's harder these days because of social media, it's almost like a bit more real life now.

"Whereas when I was a kid, after school you just kicked a ball all the time. I played five-a-side whenever I could, I went to the local youth club to have a kick about.

"My Mum would always have to come and shout me in for my dinner, but I just had a football all the time and played whenever I could."

Boyce has featured 28 times for his country, Northern Ireland and the striker admits it's the ultimate honour for any player.

"It was a massive honour. I was still in the Irish league and was part time then and at the time, players from the Irish League weren't normally selected, as the squad was very difficult to get into.

"So, it helped me in my career to get moves to other clubs to boost my profile, but also to play against the best at the highest level, as for any player that's what you want to do. You want to challenge yourself as a player and see how far you can go."

"It was a huge moment," Boyce continued, "we were in the Championship at the time, so I think people were expecting Hibs to win, but we thought we had a really good team at the time, and we thought we were confident we were going to win.

"To take the penalty and win the game, it was just massive for us. I think it was the first Edinburgh derby I started in, so it was just such a big game. It was really amazing to come out on top in that one for lots of different reasons. That one meant a lot to us all."

THE STORY OF THE SHIRTS

Hearts have unveiled a trio of stunning kits for the 2023/24 campaign.

This season's home kit begins our 150th anniversary celebrations with a nod to our deep connection with the city of Edinburgh – our home. Our traditional maroon colours shine through in the latest offering from our partnership with Umbro.

The home shirt reflects on our connection with the capital, with the shoulder and sleeve featuring a stunning design that represents the iconic cobbles that surround the Heart of Midlothian mosaic on the city's Royal Mile.

Our eye-catching away shirt features a striking pink design that links back to away colours of seasons gone by. Of course – there's the third kit, which you can read about elsewhere in the pages of this annual.

All three shirts will be available throughout the season in the Clubstore or online from Hearts Direct.

QUIZ ANSWERS

P30. WORDSEARCH

```
            M U S N E                         D E N E S
            T N Z P T F B                   C E Q Y K C I
        U V L A C O K U S I             C J I J F X U O R J
        G S X B S S B O J O Y O       W H T P Q J H Y E T A X
        B Z X M F N K U R Q X F U   Q K F B S N F X M P S I E
      Z N R Q F K W J S F Z U H H L M A Y V H B H Y Y F A D M Q H
      A R U A H A Y U Q T P L V Q P C H K T H Z R A S X E P R L N
      N G V K E O X F U X Z X P W I B F P N K M U D N O Y R Z I D
      D Q H S A N E C M W U O T Y N E C A S T L E E T K I S H Z Z
      E B M E R O A A N P H H U M D P W Q F Z S J J J Y U L L M A D
      R C L O K C R B E H L U M A X I B K I T I J O C K H A I J B
      G W F Z F A Y T J U V P G S D F A X T C B W A U U J F N T M
      E N H M Z N H I R A K G A W L T N R P Y B G C O T I Y S D R
        G H Z P V G R W J K T G O R G I E X U I F W A O O L C K
        Z T L W J X F J P I S X M J U N T Y T C X A Y J F S I X
        A L D W O H T B M G V P H I G Y R A K C W X R Q J F
        Y T I R Z K H C T Q R Q Z I Q E R I R K O T F H
        R D V M I A Y L F X R H M D A O Z B G D E H
        D E V L I N R U G S H E T G N T Z T N R
          X R L T X E Q W F B X V A E C J H M
          U N J J X R X T B S J Y I L X L
          W P D F A A U P O I A H W X
          R U S Z R S L O D H T A
          I C O W F K O X N V
          T U S F Z O R I
          I B Z R V U
          J Z C P
          C F
```

P32. MISFITS

1A	Craig Halkett		2A	Nathaniel Atkinson
1B	Peter Haring		2B	Alan Forrest
1C	Liam Boyce		2C	Craig Gordon

P33. THE HEARTS QUIZ

1. Livingston

2. Josh Ginnelly

3. Dundee United

4. Zander Clark

5. 4th

6. Ross County 6-1

7. Nathaniel Atkinson

8. Shankland, Humphrys, Ginnelly, Sibbick

9. Alex Cochrane

10. Lawrence Shankland

P31. SPOT THE BALL

WHERE'S JOCK?